"Where Have All the Jobs Gone?"

Why your job hunt strategy

isn't working

-and what to do instead!

RUTH SULLIVAN

ISBN: 1517727499
ISBN-13: 978-1517727499

"We must do away with the absolutely specious notion that everybody has to earn a living.... We keep inventing jobs because of this false idea that everybody has to be employed at some kind of drudgery because.....he must justify his right to exist. So we have inspectors of inspectors and people making instruments for inspectors to inspect inspectors. The true business of people should be to go back to school and think about whatever it was they were thinking about before somebody came along and told them they had to earn a living."
Richard Buckminster Fuller

CONTENTS   PAGE

Introduction

Are you tired of the job hunt?

Maybe you are stuck in a job you hate and desperate to escape –or unemployed and anxiously seeking *any* paid employment.

Either way, you have probably found yourself in a never –ending cycle of trawling the Situations Vacant columns, filling in long application forms, and even firing off CVs on the off-chance that someone might be hiring.

And why not? This is the method you were trained to follow –and it worked in the recent past.

So why isn't it working now?

The good news is that it's not your fault - but the world of work has changed. It hasn't disappeared - it's just gone online!

The old 20th Century workplace (huge companies staffed by hundreds or even thousands of full-time employees on one site) is being replaced by leaner, more flexible ways of doing business.

Although the *way* we work has changed, that doesn't mean that there is any *less* work!

However, the 20th Century job hunting techniques you were taught are no longer effective in the Internet Age.

There's more than enough work to go around. There are plenty of customers for your services and unlimited opportunities to earn great money doing work you love!

There's nothing wrong with **you** – but it's time for a new strategy!

Ruth Sullivan,

Bergamo 2015

Find out more here:

http://ewire24.com

CHAPTER 1

THE REVOLUTIONARY CHANGES IN THE WORLD OF WORK

Over the course of the last two or three centuries, companies expanded by leveraging the manpower of others.

In this era, which has been called 'The Industrial Age', one man's vision might require an army of employees to bring a product to the market. The construction of bricks and mortar factories and office blocks, installation of machinery and infrastructure, and everyday operation and maintenance required the presence and physical input of hundreds or even thousands in one geographical location.

The day-to-day running of huge factories and offices generated countless **job titles** – receptionists, operators, shorthand typists, fitters, electricians, canteen workers, inspectors, drivers, security guards, accountants –and layer upon layer of supervisors, managers and secretaries.

Although this period was a temporary phenomenon in human history, it lasted long enough for generations to grow up believing that employment in the service of other people was the norm. **It seemed much easier to get a job than to sit down and think how you could apply thought to developing your own creativity to work for yourself, so career choices were determined by what was required by employers.**

By the end of the 20th Century, the career strategy of 'do well at school, get good grades and find a job working for someone else' had become firmly established.

Most people didn't even think of questioning this approach, and schools are still preparing students for the mass employment of the Industrial Age.

However, by the mid-1990s, this era was already drawing to a close, as businesses began to realise the potential of the World Wide Web.

The advent of the Internet Age meant it was no longer necessary to employ so many full-time staff to run a business. As companies moved online, they became lighter and more flexible. Offline, traditional companies struggled to compete and were forced to either downsize or go out of business.

The inevitable result of fewer permanent positions on offer was increasing competition for every vacancy, leading to lower salaries as the supply of workers exceeded the demand for their services.

The immediate response of many was to blame the Internet for the loss of jobs.

This reaction arose from the perspective of the Industrial Age – **the assumption that work should be provided by someone else**.

A generation groomed to become employees, and who had grown up believing that 'other people' created work, were ill-prepared to meet the challenge of the revolutionary shift to online working.

Since they had never been shown **how** they could follow their natural talents to create their **own** work, they were not primed to appreciate the amazing **opportunities** the Internet was opening up.

They had been taught to look **outside** of themselves to design their working lives, and their **career choices were determined by the job titles on offer**- i.e. by **what employers wanted**.

In the past, if a child's natural talents didn't appear to be in demand, they might be encouraged to abandon them in favour of a more 'marketable' skill.

If you grew up in the late 20th Century, you probably assumed that this was just 'how it is', and went along with the idea that the way of the world was to adapt to fit the requirements of a job description.

This thinking ignored the importance of your unique personality and your natural aptitudes - the skills you were born with. In accepting that someone else – something outside of you - should determine your working life, you, like so many others, may have dismissed your true calling or regarded it as being of little value in the world of work.

As the job market continues to contract and there are fewer salaried positions, the inevitable result will be a return to creating our own work in line with the talents we were born with.

In future, this will be the accepted approach, but, until that time, those who haven't been shown what's really going on will continue to use the outmoded 20th Century job search strategy in the 21st Century, in an attempt to succeed in the lottery of 'winning' a full-time contract in the service of someone else.

If you hate your job, it's a sure sign that you are not

working in alignment with your innate talents and that you have handed over control of your working life to another person's design for your life.

Finding another job in another company will not resolve that issue —in fact, it may be a case of 'jumping out of the frying pan into the fire'!

If you are struggling to find any work at all, chances are that you are finding it hard to match the available job titles with the natural talents you possess.

When you can't see any correlation between what's on offer and what you would like to do, the compromise you would have to make to fit the job description is too great —and so your motivation is probably not high enough to get you there.

The Internet has **not** created unemployment. The Internet has made it possible for anyone with a broadband connection to give up jumping through hoops to satisfy the job requirements of an employer, and to stop trying to be someone they are not!

It's time to be yourself!

It's time to stop looking to other people to provide you with work.

It's time to discover how your natural genius is the key

to discovering how you can **make a great living, on your terms, by serving the world in the work you were born to do.**

CHAPTER 2

WHY INDUSTRIAL ERA JOB SEARCH STRATEGIES DON'T WORK ANYMORE

The simple fact is that employers need fewer people to run their business in the Internet Age.

The number of full-time salaried jobs is declining - and that number will continue to decrease.

So, you see it's not a question of needing more qualifications, being the wrong age, not knowing the right people, not having the right interview technique: these are simply filters used (fairly randomly!) by potential employers overwhelmed by the number of applications they receive for each advertised vacancy for a full-time salaried position.

In the Industrial Age, employers typically received a few

dozen applications for every vacancy they advertised. Jobs were quite plentiful, and so people applied for posts in their field of qualification, experience and location.

As the number of salaried posts declined, job seekers started to panic and began applying for everything and anything on offer.

Added to that, at a time when companies were moving online and requiring fewer employees, the Internet also opened up job vacancy advertising to the world!

 A job listing could now be seen by a much wider national, or even international, audience.

Rather than sift through twenty application forms to select two or three candidates for interview, today's employer might be inundated with thousands of application forms!

It's just not logistically possible for any hiring manager to read every application form, and so a filter must be applied to whittle the thousands down to manageable dozens.

One of the easiest filters to apply is an age bracket: select a range of 30 to 40 years old, and instantly eliminate a lot of work!

The employer's age range filter may have been plucked out of thin air and probably bears no relevance to the ability to do the job, but the unsuccessful candidates under 30 years old might falsely assume they were rejected as being too young, whereas those over 40 acquire the false belief that they are too old.

This effect can be seen quite clearly in the context of fast food restaurants. It's obvious to most of us that a college degree is not a requirement for flipping burgers, but it is a handy filter to help the process of elimination in selecting a candidate for the post.

The filter in itself has no meaning, but if 75% or more of the applicants are rejected without anyone even reading their application form, **the traditional job search becomes little more than a lottery.**

We all know stories about people who have spent four years studying for a degree in some academic discipline, only to end up in some routine job that could be done by anyone with a couple of minutes' training. However, it's important to keep hold of the fact that : if a graduate is employed in a particular job, it does not necessarily follow that you **need** to be a graduate to do that job!

It's vital not to lose sight of **why** jobs are scarce and to remember **why** employers have to use such random filters to select a candidate from among the many capable of doing the job.

The unsuccessful applicants must take care not to take the rejection personally. They don't see what's really going on behind the scenes. They only see the standard rejection letter –or hear nothing at all. In the absence of any feedback or explanation of the interview selection methods, they are left to make their own assumptions. They may feel that they have been judged and found wanting –when the truth may be that they haven't even had a chance to have their application considered at all!

The selection process may be only a numbers game for the employers, but it can eat at the self-belief of those unable to get beyond the first hurdle in the elimination process. They start to think:

"I'm too old."

"I'm underqualified"

"I'll never find work!"

If you have assumed one or more of these **false beliefs**, it's time to **give them up**!

The traditional job hunt has become a lottery, and

you must never take it personally!

CHAPTER 3

HOW THE INDUSTRIAL AGE CAUSED US TO LOSE CONFIDENCE IN OUR NATURAL TALENTS

Every one of us was born with a natural skill set, unique to us and designed to equip us with the ability to earn good money.

All talents are of equal importance; no talent is more or less valuable than any other.

So how did we lose sight of this knowledge during the Industrial Age? What persuaded us to give up our genius in exchange for someone else's vision?

The fact that there was plentiful employment and we could go to work for someone else without having to think how to use our natural talents, doesn't mean that those talents didn't exist.

However, since employers determined what skills they needed and assigned a monetary value to them (the salary), skills came to be **graded** by Society according to their **value** to an employer.

The 'value' of work was a fairly random combination of factors which included the job's perceived difficulty, how many years of study it required, what the salary was and how much prestige it held.

This ranking of skills meant that many ignored their natural aptitudes in the pursuit of a career that seemed more 'valuable' in the eyes of Society, even if they had little interest in that field.

You may have disregarded your unique gifts, simply because they rarely or never appeared in Job Descriptions. If you had never seen evidence of demand for a salaried 'Portrait Painter' or a 'Company Guitarist', you saw little opportunity to monetize your talent, and so your genius became a weekend hobby – or even forgotten about entirely!

You might continue to volunteer your services in an amateur capacity, but, by offering your talents for free, you may actually have assigned the value of 'zero' to the outstanding natural gift you were born with!

The grading of skills according to their value to an employer, led to the perception that a doctor was considered to be *more important* than a car mechanic, since a doctor had to study for 6 or 7 years at university and had a title. However, the Internet Age has already seen some car mechanics in London earning more than doctors, so the ranking of skills is already becoming less obvious.

In fact, the end of the Industrial Age means that our individual talents are no longer governed by the subjective judgements of that era.

The Internet has created a level playing field where all talents are equally valuable and no talent is more or less important than any other.

CHAPTER 4

HOW THE EDUCATION SYSTEM IS ADAPTING TO THE INTERNET AGE

A short response to that statement might be "slowly"!

Schools and colleges are continuing to train students in the traditional path of 'select a job title from those on offer and follow an educational path to get there'.

Rather than addressing the *root* of the problem - that the world of work is changing and the Industrial Age job hunt strategy no longer applies - schools are addressing the *result* of the problem –that there is increased competition for a dwindling supply of full-time jobs.

To give the education system the benefit of the doubt, we might suggest that it hasn't noticed the revolutionary changes the Internet has brought to the world of work, or is not yet able to offer students an alternative strategy.

A more cynical explanation might be that the *education industry* is **booming** as it promotes **more education** as the solution to **getting ahead of the competition.**

Rather than looking at how to serve the needs of **all** students leaving school in the 21st Century, schools are responding to parents' fears that their children will be left behind in the job hunt. The solution offered is to introduce *more testing,* at ever earlier ages, in order to separate the **winners** from the **losers** in the race to get the 'best' jobs.

Surely the responsibility of the education system is not to divide their charges into winners and losers, but to regard *every* pupil as talented and valuable - and equally worthy of being shown how to develop their natural aptitudes to create their own work in the Internet Age.

It also bears repeating that, if all talents are equally valuable, the Industrial Age classification of work into 'good jobs' and 'less important jobs' is no longer applicable.

After all, if you are working in alignment with your **unique** natural talents, **there is no competition.**

Less competition would mean less need for more education.

However, as the possession of a degree becomes a convenient currency to pass the filters of oversubscribed job vacancies, colleges are able to offer *more education* (at a price!) as the solution to securing a salaried post.

The consequent rise in the number of graduates does not mean there has been a rise in the number of jobs requiring a degree. In fact, it has led to the devaluation of the degree as currency, with the result that increasingly higher qualifications are required −**not** to be able to do the job, but to stand a chance of getting an interview!

CHAPTER 5

THE TRUE VALUE OF ANY WORK
(AND WHY YOU'LL NEVER GET RICH WORKING
FOR SOMEONE ELSE!)

If all of us are born with a unique set of talents, and no talent is more or less valuable than any other, how come some people are earning huge amounts of money while others struggle?

To answer that question, we must look at how work is really measured.

The **true value of any work** lies, not in man hours, but in the **creative input**.

When an employer has an idea, s/he builds the business and contributes the creativity to the enterprise – and so s/he reaps the rewards.

The employee follows instructions and gets paid for

their time. This remuneration is determined by what the employer thinks the employee's time is worth to him/her.

Our reaction might be to think that hard graft is worth more than dreaming up ideas –and, if so, we need to examine where those beliefs came from- but it doesn't alter the fact that work is not measured in terms of time, but in terms of creativity.

In the Industrial Era, when there was greater demand for, or even a shortage of, employees for hire, the going rates and benefits packages were good. This made it seem like a sensible choice, and quite an attractive idea, to go to work for someone else.

Why spend time developing creativity and designing a business model, testing and investing, when you could enter a job straight after school and get money in your hand at the end of the first week?!

The transition from completing education to receiving a steady income could be reduced to a minimum, and the promise of annual leave, sick pay and a fixed pension upon retirement became the objectives in a workforce who prized security over job satisfaction.

Not only did people want security for themselves , but they desired the same security for their children, and so generations grew up with the belief that job security, rather natural aptitude, was the main consideration when choosing a career.

By willingly handing over control of their work life and giving up job satisfaction in exchange for drudgery, millions found themselves trapped in jobs they didn't love - and out of alignment with their true purpose in life.

The belief took hold that 'this is how it is' and that 'everybody hates their job'. The word 'work' came to be associated with the torture you had to endure in order to make money. With so many hating their work, it's hardly surprising that begin to wish away the days from Monday to Friday —and live for the weekend. Some are even wishing their life away —living for retirement! How sad is that?

The job benefits packages offered towards the end of the 20th Century went some way to easing the pain of suffering a job you hated, but does that level of compensation still exist today?

Even though paid employment appeared to guarantee the security of a regular pay packet, the downside was the limited control available to the employee to increase the size of the pay packet! Of course, there might be the possibility to work extra hours to augment their basic wage, or to be promoted to a higher salary level, but their earnings were always measured in **time** –and, by necessity, limited by the number of hours in a day. The employer's earnings, however, were measured in terms of **creativity**, which is not limited by time.

As the ratio of jobs to employees continues to decrease, employers don't need to offer such competitive packages to attract staff, and so wages are stagnant or even falling.

In addition, the financial crises and low interest rates of recent years have taken their toll on pension funds, with many unsure when –or even if!- they will be able to retire!

The argument **for** working for an employer is rapidly disappearing.

Does it still make sense to sell your time to the highest bidder?

Of course, there will always be a place for paid employment, and it is a good short-term option to earn money or gain contacts and experience, but it can no longer be regarded as the 'safe' long-term option.

The Internet allows **you** to leverage the same advantages as any business or employer: low overheads, fast start up and access to the global market. You are now free to **monetize your creativity** and establish your own security!

The strategy you were taught for the 20th Century favoured the employers. Schools drew up a curriculum designed to offer a broad general education – a one-size-fits-all approach – to give the best chance of appealing to as many potential employers as possible. It seemed like a good idea to have many strings to your bow, to arm you with the best possible chance in the numbers game.

But this strategy did not take into account the enormous **value** of your unique talents. You were convinced by the argument that a limited regular salary was sufficient recompense for **giving up your birthright**!

But there is a price to pay for ignoring the gifts you were born with!

You already have your talents and the resources to express them. All you need now is **resourcefulness**.

When you take the time to learn how to develop creativity (i.e. resourcefulness) to nurture your talents, you discover how you can bring value to the world. As you add value, you receive financial reward in return.

Your gifts were given to you to be used: they are not an optional extra, but a fundamental part of who you are.

In denying your gift, you deny yourself.

If you are not earning the salary you want or deserve – ask yourself why!

The old 20th Century job hunt strategy was limited by geographical location and the requirements of an employer. It fostered the 'Jack-of-all-trades' approach to work, to permit the job search net to be spread as widely as possible. Your job hunt approach was to be "all things to all men"!

But online working puts an end to the need to have back-up plans and secondary skills and a string of certificates and qualifications. It allows you to prosper as a master in your niche.

The Internet makes it possible to communicate and trade with the world: your chances of connecting with the clients who are actively looking for your niche or specialist skills are greatly enhanced.

Whatever expertise you offer, there are people searching for it online.

Your customers are waiting for you!

When you work in alignment with your genius – your true area of expertise - there is no need to acquire everyone else's genius too!

Of course, you can –and do- have other interests outside your niche, but that doesn't mean they have to form part of your business.

If your value as an employee is on a downward spiral, and you don't have much control over that, it doesn't alter the fact that your **innate** talents never lose their value – and they are needed in the world right now. When you factor in the infinite potential of applying creativity to monetize your natural gifts –it seems blindingly obvious where your success lies!

'Getting a job' is no longer the safe option.

Why would you **want** to work for someone else?

CHAPTER 6

THE PHYSICAL TOLL OF LIVING A LIFE OUT OF ALIGNMENT WITH YOUR TRUE PURPOSE

If you were persuaded by the argument in favour of job security over job satisfaction, and abandoned the work you were born to do, you handed over control, not only of the work you do, but over the life you lead.

As a result, you find yourself spending 8 or more hours a day doing work you don't enjoy, at a location you might not choose, following the instructions of a manager whose methods you don't approve of, in the company of colleagues who are equally dissatisfied.

We all understand that paid employment is a compromise and we may be able to absorb the discomfort and inconvenience - for a while.

However, there is a physical price to be paid for living a life that's not of your design. The constant strain of bending out of alignment with your real nature and adapting to suit working conditions imposed and managed by other people eventually takes its toll.

The inevitable result is STRESS.

Stress is the physical manifestation of **lack of control** over some aspect of your life.

When coping with a stressful working environment, the sufferer will do anything to free themselves from that unbearable situation.

In fact, one of the symptoms of this stress is the desire to go on holiday. You are hardly back from one vacation until you are planning the next —and when you are asked what you would do if you had unlimited resources, the answer is usually something like 'lie on a beach for a year'!

Suffering from work stress gets little attention since it is such a common occurrence for people to tolerate a job they hate. It becomes generally accepted that everyone hates their job, so the only thing to do is to put up with it —not necessarily quietly!

We spend hours moaning about the long, unsociable hours, the low salary, the petty rules, the inconvenient working conditions, the restricted leisure time, the unreasonable bosses, the irritating colleagues, the lack of control- and yet, when we are offered the liberating opportunity to create our ideal working life in line with our natural talents and on our terms, we fail to see it for the gift it is!!

We still race to join the job hunt and beg employers to take us on, knowing that we must hand over control of how we spend our precious lives, and surrender to someone else's plan for our time.

We complain about hating our salaried employment – and yet we continue to complain when this old, defunct industrial model is taken away from us and replaced with something infinitely better – the power to design our own ideal working life on our terms!

CHAPTER 7

ARE YOU A VICTIM OF CIRCUMSTANCE OR THE MASTER OF YOUR OWN DESTINY?

The answer to that question will determine your success in life.

Victims believe in luck. They tell themselves that others are wealthy because they have an unfair advantage – they were born into a rich family or a rich country, they had an expensive education, parents with influence or useful contacts, privilege, an easy life or sheer good fortune.

By contrast, they see their own *lack* of success as a product of being born into a poor family, in a poor country, not enough education: so many disadvantages blocking their path to success.

Victims believe that life is a lottery, and that fate will deliver random results to 'lucky' people, while they, however, suffer repeated setbacks from outside circumstances beyond their control.

An Indian philosopher once pointed out that events or things themselves are neutral, but that it is the meaning we assign to the events that makes them either positive or negative.

We all have a choice.

If we **choose** to **believe** that we are successful, we will become so. If we **choose** to **believe** that the odds are stacked against us, we will continue to find evidence to support that belief.

So which set of beliefs serves us best?

Thanks to the media, we hear the stories of people who appear to have achieved fame and fortune overnight. The work to get there is a less interesting news story, and often gets left out. This adds weight to the perception that successful people just got lucky.

"The harder I work the luckier I get." Sam Goldwyn, Film Producer

In an age where we expect instant gratification, the idea of building an enterprise and working towards success can seem too much effort.

Much easier to buy a lottery ticket and wait to see where the finger of luck will point!

The universe is not random. You are not here by accident. You have a purpose to fulfil and a unique skill set and personality which is designed to get you there.

Victims tend to focus on to the negative side of news reporting that appears to prove them right and justify their inaction. The news bulletins report that there are no jobs —so the situation is hopeless.

The victim's response is to blame someone else - the Government, the employers, their age, their education, whatever, to avoid taking control of the situation.

They are **waiting for a lifeline** to get them where they want to go.

However, those who are willing to **take responsibility** for what happens in their lives, become masters of their own destiny. They don't waste time sitting around waiting for someone to throw them a lifeline: they focus on **taking action to build their own stairway to success.**

42

CHAPTER 8

FOCUS : THE KEY TO EVERYTHING

You get what you focus on.

If your focus is on lack of opportunity, disadvantage and competition, that's what you will find.

If you **believe** there is no work, you will **find** evidence everywhere to support that belief.

Your beliefs are very powerful; you get what you **believe** you will get, or, as Henry Ford put it :

"Whether you think you can, or that you can't, you're usually right."

So what if you were to change the beliefs that don't serve you and replace them with beliefs that gets you where you want to go? Would it even matter whether they were 'true' or not?

As previously mentioned, all things and events that happen are essentially without meaning; one person's interpretation may differ from another's opinion of the same incident. To a child, a heavy snowfall is an exciting and welcome reason to stay home from school and play! To a housebound elderly person, the snow might be seen as a nuisance or even a catastrophe.

The snowfall is neither good nor bad, but is **assigned meaning** by the people affected by the experience.

Consider the case of a hiring manager using a filter to eliminate a large percentage of the job application forms and make his job easier.

Regardless of whether the manager's action was 'good' or 'bad', if you didn't receive an invitation for an interview and you didn't know why (you don't actually know how the selection procedure was conducted), you **assigned** meaning to that outcome.

That meaning then enters your belief system and so your focus will then be drawn to any further evidence that proves you right. (It's a natural human trait to prefer to be *right* than to be *successful*!)

Those with a victim mentality might choose to think that they were too old or not qualified enough etc., but did that chosen belief serve them? Of course not.

However, now they are choosing to focus on what they believe are their inadequacies, and everything they see in the world of work will appear to confirm the belief they have chosen to focus on. If they believe they are too old for work, they will notice any survey which highlights the number of over 40s out of work. They will be less inclined to notice the article that proves their false assumption wrong – for example, a report that shows that employers are favouring more mature employees.

Everything that has shown up in your life so far is evidence of what you have focused on.

If your focus has been running on default mode - distracted or scattered randomly – then you are not in control of the results you see in your life.

You have actually been responsible for the results you have experienced- probably unintentionally - but, without clear instruction or focus, the outcome is likely to fall short of what you would like.

Without direction, you are like a browser at the travel agent –you may have lots of ideas of how to spend a holiday in the sun and the many wonderful options available to you, but, until you actually **decide** on a destination, you cannot take action to start planning the holiday and making it happen.

Just by being conscious of this, you can stop allowing your life to happen by accident and take control to create your life on purpose! Not by default, but by your own intention!

To do this means taking responsibility for your actions and discovering the real potential you have to set goals and reach them, simply by harnessing the power of your focus!

Evidence of the power of focus is when you learn a new word. You think you have come across it for the first time and you learn its meaning. Then, over the course of the next week or two, that 'new' word appears again and again! Of course, the word had been there all along, but it is your focus on it that has changed.

Ever noticed when you decide to buy a certain car, you start to see that make and model everywhere? There hasn't been an overnight increase in the number of those cars on the road, but your focus has been drawn to it —and suddenly it crops up everywhere!

This is what happens when you move your focus away from what you **don't** want —unemployment, poverty, lack, a job that destroys your very soul- and shift it to what you **do** want.

When you get clear about what you want in life and

where you want to go, your focus - your mind- is primed to look for the opportunities to get you there. Just like the car, the opportunities were there all along, but it is your focus on them that has changed.

That's why it's not enough to set woolly, catch-all intentions such as 'earning more money', 'having more time off', 'not being poor' —these are examples of scattered focus and will not be effective in leading you anywhere.

In order to instruct your own mind to bring you what you want in life, you must give it clear, well-defined instructions.

You must decide *exactly* what you want - it all starts with the decision!

CHAPTER 9

WHY YOUR MIND RESISTS CHANGE

We are often reminded of the power of the human brain, and how we utilize only a fraction of its potential.

The subconscious brain is much larger than the conscious brain and takes care of all the day-to-day running of the body, so that vital functions, such as heartbeat and breathing, are controlled without our conscious input. This makes sense: we would never get anything done if we had to keep remembering to instruct the lungs to breathe!

The role of the subconscious mind is to keep us safe and alive —even when our conscious minds are concentrating on other things – and, for this reason, they are quite difficult to change or re-programme. Obviously, it's not in our best interests to try to change our heart rate at will or over-ride the functions that have kept us alive up so far.

Much of the programming of the subconscious is hard-wired into your system by the age of seven or eight. Before that time you learned that fire is hot and not to touch it. You learned that bees can sting and that it's not a good idea to put your finger in the mouth of the neighbours' dog. Lessons acquired from your experiences are stored away to keep you safe.

The subconscious mind also absorbs ideas and 'facts' you are exposed to at an early age, and opinions formed before the age of seven –whether true or not- are pretty much locked into your beliefs about the world. (When I use the word 'beliefs' here, I don't mean 'religious beliefs', but the broader sense of 'what you hold to be true based on your experience of the world around you'.)

If, at this early stage, you are exposed to comments like 'work is hard', 'money is very difficult to come by', 'it's not easy to find a job' or 'you must do well at school in order to succeed in life', these are likely to form the basis of how you view the world. It's not the fault of the person you learned these ideas from – they were simply repeating the beliefs they had learned from someone else when they were your age!

If you had grown up in a family of multi-millionaires, you

probably wouldn't have been exposed to such negative opinions about work and money, and your experience of the world around you was likely to be one of wealth and opportunity. (Often when people from rich families are successful, the judgement is made that they had their success handed to them on a plate —when, in fact, all they received was the **belief** that they would succeed.)

Whatever beliefs you acquired while growing up have served you quite well so far – you're still alive! – and so the subconscious mind sees no reason to change them.

The subconscious mind resists change- in fact, for the subconscious, change equals death -and must be avoided at all costs!

If you need any evidence of this, consider how your subconscious mind sabotages your good intentions of eating healthily! Your conscious mind may have been convinced by the logical argument for eating more vegetables and cutting down on sugar.

But the subconscious mind doesn't respond well to logic!

The subconscious interest in keeping you alive will attempt to override any conscious information about good nutrition, and will arm you with a multitude of good reasons why you should eat that bar of chocolate to avoid starvation!

The same happens when you realise that your ideal working life is within your reach —and that there is no longer any necessity to sign away your working day to an employer. You start thinking of how you can design your work around your talents - and then you give up at the first hurdle, when your subconscious mind detects 'change' and convinces you that it's 'safer' just to apply for jobs and let someone else do the thinking!

That is the subtle sabotage of the subconscious —it is programmed to keep you stuck where you are!

It takes a certain amount of energy —and motivation -to get around the resistance presented by the subconscious.

When you decide what you want, and declare your intent to get there, your motivation must be stronger than the subconscious mind's tactics to prevent you moving forward.

That's why some of your job applications fail. If you are applying for a job just to get money, or simply to escape the living hell of the job you are in now, your desire to get the job is not strong enough to overcome the sabotage of your own mind.

CHAPTER 10

CHALLENGING THE FALSE BELIEFS KEEPING YOU STUCK

"The unexamined life is not worth living" Socrates

Whether your false beliefs about work and money were absorbed in your childhood, or learned in school, it may be time to question why you still hold them and whether they still serve you.

As we saw before, you may be held back **not** by external events, but by the meaning you assign to them. The situation itself is neither good nor bad, but it is your *belief* about that situation that matters.

If you believe that there is a scarcity of work and that there is no way you can earn good money – then that will become true for you.

If, however, you move your focus from your acquired beliefs about work - unemployment, low salaries, and lack of opportunity - you free yourself up to notice the **evidence** of success that challenges your beliefs.

(Your early experience with the teeth of the neigbours' dog may have caused you to grow up with the false belief that 'all dogs are dangerous'. You could hold on to that belief for the rest of your life – and live in terror of meeting a dog in the street. Or you could **allow** yourself to see the evidence that most dogs are well-behaved, and eventually let go of the belief holding you in fear.)

There are many people earning a great living in work they have designed, and who wake up in the morning and can't wait to get started.

In this age of Information, internet entrepreneurs are appearing in all sorts of niches we never dreamt of before.Teenagers are making their first million online with simple blogs and Youtube videos.

The evidence is all around you, if you look for it.

When we first set an intention to achieve a goal, we are faced by our false beliefs that tell us 'it can't be done', and list all of our perceived inadequacies. We will always find something that sets the successful person apart from us –some reason why they have an advantage that we don't.

The truth is that everyone has their own set of advantages and disadvantages, just as unique as their natural talents. If you choose to focus on the disadvantages, guess what will happen?

But, what would happen if you allowed yourself to list your advantages?

Look at the old excuses which held you back. They may have had some meaning in the framework of paid employment, but those judgements no longer matter.

For example, take the false beliefs 'I'm too old' or 'I'm over 65' – the concept of a retirement age does not depend on an individual's ability or desire to work, but is a relic from the Industrial Age, when retirement was seen as a blessed release from the accumulated stress of being trapped in a job you hated for 20, 30 or 40 years!

People are living longer, healthier lives –lives that will be even longer and even healthier when free of the stress of doing jobs they are not meant to be doing!

If you are absorbed in work you love and love the work you're doing –why would you want to retire?

CHAPTER 11

OVERCOMING RESISTANCE TO PLANNING

Fail to plan, plan to fail.

We all know that planning is effective, and yet less than 5% of the population actually take the time to sit down and draft a plan for their life.

It is worth noting that most of the people who are high achievers and are earning good money in work they love are in that 5%!

Some people love planning and really enjoy designing a fishing trip, a city tour or a wedding. They draw up lists of things to be done so that every minute of the day is accounted for, and yet the astonishing fact is that they have probably **don't** have a plan for their life.

If we understand the value of planning, why do we put

up such resistance to it?

The word 'planning' may have unpleasant associations with a tedious work environment that involves duty, chores, deadlines and an inflexible schedule.

Planning seems to exclude the excitement of spontaneity : we feel restricted and worry that we might miss out on the joy of life by over-organizing it!

The inadequacy of language means that 'planning' *sounds* too much like hard work, and our resistance to it means we find excuses to avoid it – I'm too busy to plan!

But what if we looked beyond the language to see what we actually do when we plan the future. Our conscious mind acts on written orders and logical reasoning, and can be trained to follow a sequence of instructions.

However, the more powerful subconscious mind doesn't respond well to words and reasoning, and, as we discussed earlier, resists anything that might bring about change!

The subconscious works better when presented with images, sounds and feelings –and so this is the most effective way to get it onboard and instruct it to bring you what you want.

Again, language doesn't serve us well here –for the

word we use for messages in pictures, sounds and feelings is 'dreaming'. We are taught to associate 'day dreaming' with 'unrealistic imagining' and to feel guilty about 'wasting' time, when we could be bashing about getting things done! When you see how powerfully dreaming impacts the subconscious mind and gets it to cooperate with our intentions, a better description of the task would be **'realistic** imagining'.

This is a technique we already use, without thinking about it, whenever we need to overcome the resistance of the subconscious mind.

For example, the conscious mind is convinced by the argument that going to the gym every Monday would be a great way to tone muscle and shape up - and so you have willingly signed up to an annual gym membership.

When it gets to Monday evening, it's raining, you're tired and hungry and the subconscious is bombarding you with images of why you should give the gym a miss. You visualize yourself sinking into a comfortable chair in front of the warm fire, you smell the delicious casserole coming out of the oven and see your favourite programme just starting on television.

This is how the subconscious mind powerfully communicates ideas to keep you out of the gym and stuck in the safety of your sedentary lifestyle.

The most effective way to counter these powerful messages is to reply to the subconscious using the same technique of pictures and feelings. You send it images of how saint-like you will feel after your workout, the hot bubble bath, and how your good work will allow you to enjoy a guilt-free dessert after dinner.

You see: you already know **how** to speak to the subconscious to get it to cooperate with your conscious intentions.

So it's only a matter of using those same techniques to get the subconscious onboard to take you where you want to go.

Instead of writing out your plans in pencil to submit to the subconscious, you have the more powerful - and less resistant- option of using your imagination to show your own mind exactly what you want by demonstrating your future ideal life in as much detail as you can visualize.

Your wonderful future in glorious technicolor! What's not to like?

The more you exercise this form of communication with the subconscious mind, the more effectively it will respond to bring your vision (i.e. plan!) into reality.

Just remember to keep a written note of your plans as evidence that they are coming into effect —otherwise, how can you measure your success?

"What gets measured gets done."

If you keep a journal of your plans and note down your goals, together with your successes, mistakes and triumphs, you will collect evidence to prove to yourself that you are moving forward.

Instead of undefined statements, such as "I did *better* than last year", you will have a real, quantifiable record of your progress, such as "My client list grew by 45% in two months".

Ruth Sullivan

CHAPTER 12

THE BEST JOB FOR YOU!

It should be obvious by now that the work you were born to do is the best work for you!

When you realise this, you start thinking "How could it be any other way?"

The skill comes naturally to you, and so other people may struggle to do it as well as you can.

Your natural skills are things you enjoy doing. If you work at what you love doing, it doesn't seem like work – you would do it anyway, even if you didn't get paid. (N.B. that doesn't mean you should undervalue your gift or do it for free – remember: you were given that gift in order to make a good living and earn money!)

Do you undervalue your skill because it comes so easily to you –and you assume that it comes equally easily to other people?

Have you undervalued your skill because you haven't seen it in the form of a job title?

Don't allow your talent to be judged by the ranking system of the Industrial Age.

Your genius is something inherent in you – it will never be forced by someone else's design for your life or by Society's artificial –and changeable! – perceptions of prestige or difficulty.

A parent or grandparent's dream for you to become a doctor is *their* dream! *You* are the person who has to live with the consequences of that decision, and, if it's the wrong choice for you, you may have a lifetime of regret and stress to deal with. Your older family member's wishes for you probably stem from the perspective of their generation, when doctors were perceived to have the best opportunity to achieve prestige and high earnings potential, from among the job titles on offer.

You are now living in the post-Industrial Age, and you are not limited by job titles or the expectation that you have to be employed by someone else. You have limitless potential to develop your own unique skill set to achieve great things.

Don't confuse what you CAN do with what you SHOULD be doing. All of us are competent in many things other than our natural genius, but the need to operate one of your secondary talents in order to find work is a relic of Industrial Age thinking.

It is much faster and more effective to take something you are really good at and develop it to become an expert your niche, than to constantly struggle to upgrade something you are quite good at. If you are 'quite good', there will always be others who are naturally gifted in that field, and you will have to work hard to reach and maintain the level of competence that comes effortlessly to them.

As the cost of a college degree –in terms of finance, time and lost earnings - continues to rise, it is inevitable that we will have to get back to considering the **purpose** of further education –and what we **need** (as opposed to **want**) a degree for.

There are certain professions, such as Law, Medicine, Engineering, for which a degree is a necessary requirement, and those professions continue to recompense the graduate for their time spent studying the subject.

However, if you have no desire to enter a profession that requires 4 or 5 years of expensive further education, why do you want to go to college?

If you are nurturing your natural talents to bring you success and wealth and the lifestyle you desire, where would further education fit into the plan? If you are your own boss and decision-maker, what difference would the title of 'graduate' make to your work life?

These are major questions to consider before committing yourself to more years of study and a huge bank loan before you start earning any money.

If you want to study for the sheer pleasure of immersing yourself in a topic you enjoy, there will be plenty of opportunities to do that later, when you are financially secure. You don't even need to relocate to a college campus, if you don't want to: there are many online degree programmes available. The UK Open University allows you to do a fully accredited degree programme from anywhere in the World, with attendance in person only required for a week or two in a calendar year.

The fact that this low-cost option is not yet popular amongst school leavers suggests that many are choosing to go to University for the social life –an expensive long-term holiday to put off what they see as the inevitable drudgery of getting a job! Part of the cost of this expensive indulgence may be funded by Mum and Dad – as long as Mum and Dad have been convinced by the 20th Century argument that a degree is the necessary route to secure employment!

The value of a degree as currency, to get a head start over the competition in the job market, is diminishing and an expensive, high-risk strategy.

In purely logistical terms, it is worth examining the ROI - Return on Investment- against whatever reasons are motivating you to enter tertiary education.

For example, if the cost of a degree is roughly equivalent to 2 years of a full-time salary, and you spend 4 years in full-time study, you lose 6 years of income.

Because professions regarded as prestigious (under the Industrial Age grading system!) require a degree, don't assume that a degree automatically confers prestige on a job – or even on you!

You are free of this outmoded judgement of people or professions - which only made any sense in an era when everyone was thinking in terms of their value to a potential employer.

The purpose of a degree -expensive extra training required for a profession that needs lots of accumulated knowledge before you start – has been lost, as the 'labels' of 'graduate' or 'non-graduate' have fueled Society's craving to set up a judgement-based ranking system.

This division is meaningless in itself – and is only important if YOU or someone else gives it meaning.

The possession of a degree does not imply anything about the intelligence or value of an individual. It may say that the person was willing to forego income and take on massive debts in order to study a subject of which they might use 10% or nothing at all in their profession.

In fact, as many recent graduates have noticed to their cost, it is only after graduation, when they start looking for a job, that they discover that a degree is no longer a passport to a well-paid job.

If you have a degree, it is worth reflecting on how much of the knowledge you gained in college you have actually used in your working life. What has been the ROI in your career?

If you don't have a degree – are you using this perceived 'lack' as an excuse to hold you back, or for not going where you want to go?

Many entrepreneurs don't have degrees. A degree, like anything else, should be measured against its worth in getting you where you want to go.

If it doesn't affect your chosen direction, then a degree is an expensive optional extra.

Many subjects can now be studied at depth online. Perhaps in future, most degrees will be awarded online —otherwise vast numbers of people will struggle to survive financially.

Look again at the education industry — why is it selling the idea of a degree or a Masters as the passport to your future? Remember that it *is* an industry, and you are the potential *client*.

Being accepted on a degree course is no guarantee that you will find a relevant job at the end of it.

Universities are **not** charitable institutions in the business of helping you to find work. They are in the business of **selling** you an expensive product: a degree costs around the same as a new car.

A car salesman might offer you good finance to buy the shiny, new Mini in front of you, and tell you that it's the best investment you could ever make. But why would you take out a loan to buy a Mini, if you already have a Mercedes parked in your garage? (Work out the analogy!)

You are the ultimate judge of whether or not you need the product.

If you don't *need* it, but you still *want* it, ask yourself whether it is best to do it *now* – or would you enjoy it more when you have the money in the bank to pay for it!

CHAPTER 13

(RE-)DISCOVERING YOUR GENIUS

Some of the worst advice young people get is to be told they can do anything. The limitless options to do 'anything' often obscure the 'something' they should be doing.

For some people, the 'something' —their special talent — is obvious, and they have spent their lives trying to work out how to use their genius to earn a good living.

For others, there genius is less apparent or more difficult to define. Their real talents may have been pushed to one side or buried under a new identity the owner has assumed (to make them more appealing to the job market!).

Maybe you are a natural storyteller and longed to write, but that passion got lost when you decided that studying

Law would bring you a secure and well-paid career. You now *identify* yourself as a lawyer, and that might make it hard to remember what you really wanted to do.

Your true purpose will be something that you love doing and an idea that fills you with joy.

Forget the misconception that work must be hard and unpleasant —these are assumptions derived from the Industrial Age model, when you were encouraged to give up your true calling in order to earn money in the service of someone else's calling.

Be wary, too, of confusing your favourite hobby with your life's work! Your calling will require you to be of service or to create something to add value to people's lives. Unless you are a professional standard golfer that people will pay to watch, your calling is unlikely to be as a golfer —although you may want to be a caddy, tournament organizer, etc

Sometimes it's hard to recognize your talent among the many abilities you have or have developed. It's helpful to consider that learned or developed skills take more effort. Your natural talents come easily to you.

In fact, because your gift comes to you so effortlessly, you might assume that it comes just as easily to everyone —and so you don't recognize it as anything special and don't consider it to be of any value.

Underestimating your value and the demand for your services stems from the 20th Century constraints of physical location –when it was much harder to communicate with the international market.

Consider the concepts of the 'penniless artist', the 'amateur' writer, the 'resting' actor, the weekend chef, the talented, but starving, busker. These labels held meaning when someone's genius had only a limited target audience in a fixed geographical area. With the ability to connect online, the unpaid talent with 'limited local appeal' can now reach out to their 'tribe'-their potential client base – located anywhere in the world.

I recently learned of someone who earns his living teaching people how to tie animal balloon shapes. What are your pre-conceived ideas about his potential market? Do they still hold any meaning when you discover he earns over a million dollars a year?

Are the stereotypes really true – or only your beliefs about them? After all, we all know the names of plenty of people who have become millionaires as actors, musicians, artists, chefs, writers etc.

Whatever your gift, if someone else can succeed in your field, then you can too!

Someone may be well aware of his or her unique gifts but can't see a way to monetize them. Without the example of someone else who has been successful in that field, they need evidence to 'know' that it is possible for them.

Remember that absence of evidence is not evidence of absence!

If Steve Jobs had told his career advisor that he wanted to create the iPad, what do you think the response would be?

If you can't see your creative potential yet, don't worry! You haven't been trained to look for it and your focus has been diverted to the jobs in existence, rather than to developing your unique talents.

The really exciting thing to discover is that creativity can be learned and practiced! The more you develop your creativity muscle, the more ideas you get - and the more creative you become. So don't be concerned if you can't see a way to utilize your talents yet – the 'how to do it' must come after the 'what to do'.

The first step is to identify your genius.

CHAPTER 14

ASKING THE RIGHT QUESTIONS
-SETTING YOUR MIND TO WORK FOR YOU

When you discover the value in nurturing your natural gifts, the conscious mind starts working on the 'what can I do?' while being sabotaged simultaneously by the subconscious fretting about 'how can I do that?'

Don't allow your focus to be split – it is important to give your full, uninterrupted attention to really knowing the "What", *before* going to work on the "How".

(Remember how, previously, your working life was governed by addressing the 'how' to make a living from the job titles on offer, *before* you even had time to figure out 'what' your purpose was?)

Don't allow the process to be hampered by your subconscious trying to solve the 'how' at the same time!

If you don't get the 'what' (the destination) right, any attempt to implement the 'how' will be in the **wrong direction**!

The following questions are practical exercises designed to get you working on uncovering your true purpose, unhindered by thoughts of how to implement it.

Don't allow your mind to run away with you just because you can see a possible route, and don't stop examining a possibility when your subconscious mind thinks it has found an insurmountable block.

Keep going and give yourself as much time as you need.

It's time to devote time to the most powerful weapon in your armoury –applied thought.

We underestimate thought –because it looks like we're not doing anything! We have been so conditioned to keep busy in physical graft, that time spent in contemplation looks lazy! In fact, our fear of being labelled physically lazy is much greater than any fear of being mentally lazy.

It has been said that Donald Trump spends around three hours a day just thinking!

Our traditional idea of work might make us resentful of someone sitting quietly in their office while we run around getting things done. However, that time devoted to thought is what develops the creativity to earn billions while the grafters are earning thousands.

Thought is way more valuable than physical work, because it is thinking that develops creativity.

If your beliefs about work have depended on the value of the man hours you can provide, then your earning potential has been limited by time.

Creativity is not bounded by time, but is the key to multiplying your value to the world and, as a result, your financial reward.

So, is it worth your while to spend some time in structured thought? By structured, I mean setting yourself a task to solve and asking your mind to show you how you can solve it. In other words, learning to ask yourself the right questions.

When people first sit down to think, they are often distracted by other things and are not used to sitting quietly. How often do we use the TV or the car radio to avoid being alone with our thoughts?

If we are serious about discovering the answers to the questions we are asking ourselves, it figures that we must allow time to receive the answers!

The following are a list of questions to help you guide your thought process to uncover your genius. The answers should not be limited by the size of the blank spaces in between!

Take your time: the purpose is not to finish the book, but to really get to the truth of what you should be doing to bring you the income and lifestyle you deserve.

Questions to help you find your real talents and purpose:

1. What do you love doing so much that it makes you lose track of time? (Make a list – the more information you uncover, the better.)

(Consider which things might be more suited to serving the world and which are purely recreational pursuits to enjoy –N.B. the difference is not always clear, but that's fine for now!)

2.What did you love doing as a child?

What did you think you would like to do when you grew up?

Why did you decide against this choice?

3. How have you chosen the jobs you have done so far? If you haven't worked before, what work would you like to do-and why?

4. Which people do you most admire and why? (You notice the qualities **you** value when you see them in other people.)

5.. Whose job would you like to do –and why? (Be honest with yourself-is it for the money, respect or contacts they have? If so, acknowledge that and consider whether you are actually interested in their work or the rewards their work brings. If it's the rewards, consider ways you could receive those rewards in work more in line with your personality and talents.)

6. If you had millions in the bank and all your family were supported, how would you spend your day?

(Note: if you are suffering from the accumulated stress of being in a job you don't like, the answer to this question is likely to include a long period of rest and doing nothing. That's OK –just factor in a long holiday, then think what you would do when you were bored of sitting on the beach- yes, it's possible!)

7. What are you good at?

These are things that people regularly ask for your help or advice on, or the good skills your parents, teachers or friends identified in you.

Make a list, then eliminate the things you find a chore: your true purpose will be something you enjoy doing.

8. What do your friends and family **say** you are good at?

Hint: Ask them!

This is important-sometimes we don't recognize a skill or talent in ourselves because it comes so easily to us, we assume that it is the same for everybody. (Be careful when a spouse or parent suggests you are good at washing up: there's an ulterior motive there!)

CHAPTER 15

IT ALL STARTS WITH THE DECISION

"If you don't know where you're going, any road will take you there" **Alice in Wonderland**

When you take the time to decide what you really want to do, you know where you are going and you can start to design your future and take the action to implement that vision in your life.

(Note: If don't take the time to choose what you want in life, then that is also a decision – you have decided **not** to choose. By giving up responsibility for what turns up in your life, you have chosen to be a victim, at the mercy of the default setting, and life will continue to seem like a random series of events over which you have no control!)

With a decision and a plan, your success is inevitable.

How powerful is that?

You are no longer distracted by the random noise of misinformation, scaremongering and negativity around you; your focus is fixed on your destination.

You start to see evidence of receiving what you focus on: suddenly opportunity seems to appear from nowhere. It was there all along, but without focus, your mind didn't see it.

Your mind is now primed with clear instructions, and it becomes an incredibly powerful instrument to bring you what you want!

Be conscious of the spanner in the works – the attempts of the subconscious mind to sabotage change and keep you stuck where you are. Examine the old false beliefs it throws at you to try to prevent you from moving forward and out of your comfort zone.

Do these false beliefs still serve you?

And who would you be if you decided to let them go?

Don't waste time regretting the decisions you made in the past. You made those decisions based on the information available to you at the time – the accepted wisdom of the Industrial Age.

It's not your fault that you were diverted from your true

purpose, or that no-one showed you how to develop and use your natural gifts.

The past is over and you can't change it.

But the past has no influence on the future you are now free to create.

PRACTICAL NOTES

If you are in a job that you don't love, but you need the money, it's obviously a sensible idea to stay there while you work on uncovering your genius and developing your potential. Your paid employment may restrict your time, but your mind is still your own to develop your creativity to use your natural talents to serve the world around you.

If you are unemployed and job seeking, it's not easy to go through the motions of continuing to apply for jobs with a view to getting interviews, but you have the advantage of being able to set aside time to focus on your real purpose and to start that journey towards what you really want to do.

What gets measured gets done and it's important to record your progress, so set a reasonable date when you expect to be free of the job search struggle or the job you don't love.

This serves two purposes –it gives you a tangible goal to work towards and shows your mind that there is a very real solution and limit to your current situation – the light at the end of the tunnel

THE NEXT STEP......

It is my express wish for you that you have found answers and inspiration in this book.

The answers often open up more questions, and inspiration without action leads nowhere. It is not my intention to leave you alone with good ideas and no support!

It is normal, when wondering 'what' to do, to be met with the subconscious mind's response of 'how', not to mention several 'buts'!

Don't allow yourself to get overwhelmed by these responses – instead, look on them as gifts – your creativity is already waking up and making enquiries!

Most people go through life in a waking sleep, allowing their future to happen **to** them; in fact, 95% of the population have never taken the time to sit down and draft a plan for their life.

If you have started by working on the questions at the end of Chapter 14, you are already on your way to taking charge of what turns up in your life. You have chosen NOT to be a victim of circumstance.

Your gifts are needed by the world and your customers

are waiting for you.

Your success will happen. The only unknown factor is how quickly it comes to you –and that is within your control.

To ensure that you stay motivated and keep on the right path to your goals, be sure to sign up here:

http://ewire24.com

This will mean you are on my mailing list to receive regular updates, tips and articles.

I look forward to hearing your feedback and answering any questions you have on the material.

To your inevitable success!

Ruth

Ruth@ewire24.com

Where Have All the Jobs Gone?